In the Roots

poems by

Abby Wheeler

Finishing Line Press
Georgetown, Kentucky

In the Roots

Copyright © 2021 by Abby Wheeler
ISBN 978-1-64662-613-7 First Edition
All rights reserved under International and Pan-American Copyright Conventions. No part of this book may be reproduced in any manner whatsoever without written permission from the publisher, except in the case of brief quotations embodied in critical articles and reviews.

ACKNOWLEDGMENTS

Women Writing for (a) Change has been a source of fellowship, and support and safety in writing, without which these poems—or any, probably—would never have been written. Laurie Lambert, your heartfelt guidance and encouragement is invaluable; thank you! Jon, thank you and I love you for telling me every poem is a "good one"—but also for being my first reader, and a smart one at that. And gratitude, always, to and for my family.

Publisher: Leah Huete de Maines
Editor: Christen Kincaid
Cover Art: Abby Wheeler
Author Photo: Abby Wheeler
Cover Design: Elizabeth Maines McCleavy

Order online: www.finishinglinepress.com
also available on amazon.com

Author inquiries and mail orders:
Finishing Line Press
PO Box 1626
Georgetown, Kentucky 40324
USA

Table of Contents

January Prayer 1

Self-Portrait 2

The Garden 3

When There Are No Sidewalks 5

Passenger Seat 6

Bottomless 7

Abundance 8

It Takes Twelve Seconds to Beat Egg Whites Fairly Stiff
at Home with a Mixer 9

Resolution 11

The Turning Point 12

Native Growth 13

Your Mother, Yourself 15

Everything I Know 16

The Girls 17

On the Lake, in Montana 18

Gold on Gold 19

Tomato Intentions 20

Meditations on a Token that Is a Seed 21

That Letters Make Words 23

Uncaged 25

I See Her in All the Places She Isn't 26

At the Rothko Chapel the Day Before 28

One Day Begins the Greening (It's in the Roots) 29

This was for me

January Prayer

Let me walk through this season
in slippered feet
over cold, planked floors

with the slow cadence of waking.
Let me drink tea with lemon and honey
first, while the shadows are soft.

Assure me that the time
for bursting will come
and that it is right, now, to rest.

Hold me, please, in the cupped palm
of absence, that I may take form
like the bear in her den

and let me know, as she does,
that darkness is a condition
of the beginning. Send to me

the god of gates and transitions
whose two faces gaze forward
and behind and block from my ears

the sirens' call to be new now.
Grant me the presence of stillness
spiked with the salty smell

of the thin, shimmering line
where the rocks meet the sea.
Remind me of the sea.

Remind me, too, of all that lies
yet unseen, beneath the dry grass
beyond the back door.

Self-Portrait

I used to take pictures on black and white film
and print them in a dark room
on paper made of silver.
I'd slip the blank sheet into the chemicals
and watch the image arrive slowly

like someone I've always known
walking the long road home.

I wanted to see the heart emerge
on my arm like that—isn't
to is—
but the artist's hand
was in the way, and besides
I was pinned on my back with you
at my bedside
talking softly, stroking the arm

that didn't have a needle in it
just like all those times before
but without the sadness and fear.

The Garden

She'd wanted to raise flowers
like other girls wanted to raise
children. When the garden
began growing in front of the little
blue house, her first, she would've
called the wild green mess perfect,
if it had been hers. If she recognized
the faces of the strangers sprouting
in her space.

The next summer, she tore it all out.
The weeding sessions became therapy,
a merciless eradication of crabgrass,
spiderwort and someone's beloved
rosebushes. In the fog of summer heat
and radiated ovaries, everything
too messy to live with was uprooted.
It had been there long enough.

That winter, the garden bed
sat under black trash bags
spread out and held down
with bricks to keep the light
from reaching it. Every day,
during the few short hours
of daylight, she'd look out
the window and be reminded
of all that was gone before it began;
dead before ever getting a chance
to live.

This summer, the garden's and
her third, is for claiming it.
Giving it a name.
Underneath the dark cover,
a few leggy weeds had grown.
Devoid of chlorophyll, they were
white, alien and strange, like toothed
sea creatures at the bottom of the ocean.
As she gently pulled them, she whispered
to the earth: I hear you. You are always a mother.

Today, the garden is alive. Bees and butterflies
find food and water, and songbirds
perch on swaying stems. She tends to it,
she imagines, like the woman before her
tended her roses. Larkspur, cosmos,
coreopsis and asters call out their names.
They are hers, and the earth's,
and there are no favorites.

When There Are No Sidewalks

We own the streets.
When it stops raining, after dinner
we come out slowly,
palms upward,
made new.
(Or maybe,
if we're young
and bursting,
we fly out the door
into the damp
like fish with wings,
no need to be made new, yet.)
We swim down the middle of the street
when there are no sidewalks,
flanked by outlines of houses
that wear the fog like a uniform,
details lost, but unimportant.
Birds and bugs resume
their chirps, hums and buzzes.
Rabbits rustle the bushes.
A woman and her dog approach,
offer a wave, a wag.
Figures on porches nod their heads
to us as we press on.
We are the members of the
church of steaming streets,
writing the verses
of our own good book
with each step.
Above us, the sky glows;
grows pink clouds,
casting a holy light
on our streets:
this kingdom
the rain gave us.

Passenger Seat

When we talk about
whatever it is we're doing,
there's no master plan;
no mountains to scale
or lists of cities whose
sunsets we'll see.
No horizon. Just grinding.
I know recovery happens
one day at a time.
Sometimes, though,
I wonder what
you're recovering.
Where's the half-buried
stepping stone you'll pull up
from the muck to uncover
your go-ahead? Your all-good.
Your plan, you tell me,
is to love me. As if
this were the greatest
devotion. As if I wasn't in the car
with the motor running
and a bagful of snacks.

Bottomless

Sometimes, I reach
into the cupboard and pull out a pot
full of stories I've never heard. Like this
tiny spoon I've been using
to nurse my cat back to health.
Did you use it
to feed one of your babies?

Abundance

Thanksgiving, and the ground is littered
with fertility. Acorns, maple helicopters,
the little winged seeds of sycamore trees
ready to seep into the earth and make
their mother proud. They say trees talk
to each other; reach out their root tips
and send messages through the fungus
in the ground. Share nutrients
and sunlight, search for kin and form
alliances with neighboring species, warn
distant relatives of disease and drought,
all without saying a word. I'm thinking
about this as we unload the car. Filling my
arms with pie and flowers for the hostess and
thinking about this ubiquitous brown, these bits
and scraps of nature who have grandparents,
aunts and uncles waiting for them, whole forests
of family to greet them and show them how to find
the sun and protect them from harm, and I'm trying
not to crush the next generation with my boots
on the way inside. There is no form to our gathering
at first, as we say hello and nibble on cheese and
crackers, but soon we take our seats: the oldest
at the top, brothers, sisters, cousins spreading
down the long walnut slabs, a cluster of smaller
tables just there. And in the moment after we've
set down our forks and leaned back in our chairs,
before we stand up and ask, *What now*?, I can
almost feel my feet grow into the ground, and
my skin turn rough so that I don't need words
to say, *There are no acorns here*;
so that I don't need ears to hear.

It Takes Twelve Seconds to Beat Egg Whites Fairly Stiff at Home with a Mixer

We wake slowly,
stretching our muscles in the animal way
you do after having slept on the ground,
rubbing out of our eyes the dust that gathers
overnight, outside, with nowhere to be
but here, and nothing to do
but whatever we feel like,
which is, for me, to close my eyes a little
longer and touch my foot to yours,
stretch my arm across your bare belly as,
perhaps, a way of pinning you in place;
draw my knee over top of your knee,
so our shins cross like wires, and you forget for now your way
of bringing the kettle to a whistle before your eyes
are fully open, before you've had a chance to decide
whether you're really ready to be awake. And it seems to work,
or maybe our brains, being so close, as it were, to the ground,
have picked up the signals that bounce back and forth
between the roots of the trees,
have temporarily forgotten the concept of "time to get up."
I wasn't being serious about that last part, of course,
but then the acorns begin dropping onto the tent,
tiny thumps, one after another,
and I'll be if it isn't as if those old oaks are telling us: *Time to get up.*
Not being ones to defy an old oak, we rise,
and you begin to bring the kettle to a whistle
and I stumble about a bit, probably read a poem—
"An Ode to Sleeping in My Clothes," maybe,
which, now that I think about that,
is particularly apropos to this particular morning, except,
as it turns out, despite the lightness of tone,
the weight that hangs beneath its words,
almost out of view,
but which makes the paper just heavy enough
to keep the page from turning just yet…
And so I rise, for the second time this morning,
and scoop into a bowl some yogurt and ricotta cheese,

the cheese out of a paper cup covered with foil
that we'd sweet-talked the cashier at the pizza place into selling us,
the night before, after our four slices and a salad.
Then I separate three eggs, add the yolks,
and dump it all into the bowl of flour, sugar, baking soda and salt
that I'd pre-mixed at home, just before I said to you,
Remind me to bring the ricotta
and then I take a clean fork and begin
to beat the whites of the eggs until they are fairly stiff but not dry.
I stand by the picnic table and whip the fork back and forth,
watch a furry caterpillar with two large black eyebrows
scooch down the side. I wander to the firepit and stop beating
long enough to rearrange the burnt black logs that I'd spread apart the night before,
having climbed out from under the sheet, nervous over the image of the flames
dancing on the side of the tent, and blow into the base, while trying to keep ashes
from drifting into the eggs. They are beginning to foam, and I keep beating
while you turn the bacon and even still while it cools and crisps
on a plate and you sit down with your book and second cup of coffee
and I keep beating for a period of time that I can't account for,
that drifts into the canopy and out into the open air beyond the cliffs
a quarter mile past our campsite (#35). And so we simply exist in these moments
that bring us a little closer to the beginning, while I whip the fork through the foamy egg whites
into a state that is certainly not dry, possibly not even stiff, and then fold them anyway
into the big bowl of flour and yolks and ricotta cheese and you place a bookmark
between open pages and scoop it all, one cupful at a time, onto the stove,
and we eat them with maple syrup—only maple syrup because I forgot to cut up a banana—
and bacon on the side while the logs burn without a flame,
and we realize all the other campers have gone,
patted their trunks shut and drove off to the next adventure, or home,
and we eat our pancakes and look at the fire and look at each other.

Resolution

Get up
the first time
the alarm sounds
and sit
next to you
as the room
fills with light.

The Turning Point

It was impossible to say exactly when it happened:
When the sun rose, she saw the thread-thin tendril
of the sweet pea pointing ambiguously any old way.
And by the time the big pink circle sank,
that little finger had wrapped itself so tightly
around its destiny, she couldn't help but nod
and resolve to do the same.

Native Growth

1. The question is how to mourn the loss of something too precious to name.

2. I'm in the garden, digging. Putting native plants in the ground.

3. I used to look out the car window as we passed hills and rivers, and imagine what this place looked like before we got here. Edit: present tense. I still do it. I've never mourned that buzzing brilliance. That "natural state" in the true meaning of the phrase, that was everything we need(ed), nothing less, and so much more. Never made my peace, because how do you let go of something never in your grasp to begin with? But I do know that everywhere I go is a little bit ruined. I resent that I got stuck with the burning blacktop, and I hate that my blood is responsible for it.

4. How do I mourn something I never knew? is what I'm thinking as I dig holes and fill them with plugs of pachysandra and tiarella. I'm starting the restoration in a dark inverted corner outside the kitchen, underneath the air conditioning unit. The disregarded, out-of-sight patch was nothing but debris and overgrown ivy. "Nothing but": as good a place as any to begin recovery.

5. I want to grieve the land, yes, but before that I'd like to grieve myself. Edit: Would not like to. Need to.

6. There's something about turning up the earth that fosters mental clarity. The physical exertion, and the rhythm of pushing, shoveling, moving, pulling, probably. Tearing it apart in order to rehabilitate it. Is that too on-the-nose? The surgeon told me a human body is just a bunch of movable parts. "Just call me Frankenstein," I said. "I mean Frankenstein's monster."

7. This little rectangle of earth which has become—in this iteration of this world—my responsibility, was once lively, full and productive. It flourished and provided and was razed and I never knew it, and I can't not think about this body of mine.

8. The soil here remembers. I'm planting something native in this empty space; something that belongs here. The question is: What belongs in the space left in me?

Your Mother, Yourself

It's not that you don't like kids. It's just that, unlike lots of girls, you never *knew* you'd be a mother. Never felt that you wouldn't be whole until you gave birth or, at least, raised a child. So, on the morning of your first radiation treatment, when the doctor said, *You're aware that your ovaries may be affected, right?*, and you *weren't* aware, you felt more stunned than sad. And then when they took out your uterus, you were like, *I get it.* It's just, people like to choose for themselves. Anyway, you honestly don't think about it too much now; there are so many other things to think about. The hardest part, the part you can't get away from, is how much moms love their kids. They have to, to get through all the cries and spills and tumbles and betrayals and still, actually love them. You can't help feeling that the love is too big for you to get close. That they don't want to say it, but are thinking, *You'll never know what it's like to live completely for someone else.* Which can hurt. Most moms are too kind to ever actually say it. But if they did, you'd probably go, *You're right, Momma. I won't.*

Everything I Know

My mom told me that she doesn't like going to sleep without knowing where all her kids are. The three of us have been a lot of places, but the worst, she said, was when my brother was in the African bush and would go weeks without checking in. Even though she prefers to be at home, all of us under her roof, she visited us everywhere, from Colorado to Peru. She chaperoned school trips to New York and DC, went to Alaska on business, and took the swim team to Orlando. She went to Africa, too—Kenya—in college. One time, she said, she got back to her tent and found a cheetah in it. Growing up, my mom wouldn't take us to the zoo, because she couldn't stand seeing the animals in cages—polar bears and big cats pacing, snakes curled up with no room to stretch out, and gorillas with their backs to us, so we can't see the family resemblance.

The Girls

You don't have my nose or my smile.
I didn't teach you to tie your shoes or blow bubbles
and I'll never be your first phone call.
But you watch me light the candles
every time you eat dinner at my table
and for just a moment
I see the flame in your eyes.

On the Lake, in Montana

Outside, the rain falls,
steady as sodality
                drips
through ancient evergreens.

Steady as sodality,
the icy river pulses
through ancient evergreens.
Nearby, men crack and thaw;

the icy river pulses,
ensuring nothing is ever the same.
Inside, men crack and thaw:
We need each other.

Ensuring nothing is ever the same,
you look at me with wet cheeks.
We need each other.
The truth older than evergreens echoes as

you look up with wet cheeks.
Drip.   Drip.   Drip.
The truth older than evergreens echoes as
outside, the rain falls.

Gold on Gold

The best thing I can imagine
(which also happens to exist)
is a goldfinch
perching on the stem
of a sunflower.

Gold on gold,
the stuff of fairytales,
currency of the gods.

Occasionally I am tempted,
like those early conquistadors,
backs broken by the weight
of bottomless treasure chests,
to be lured by siren calls
of fantastic rainbow feathers
in distant damp forests,
seductive jungle screeches,
glistening wings
on steamy mountaintops,
teeming with colors
I've never seen.
Worlds that must
surely outshine
these fields of corn
and tobacco.

But then, in the morning,
I brush my teeth
and look out the window
at sparkling wings.

Tomato Intentions

Summer is sitting
on my counter
top. It is a red tomato,
growing plumper
by the day. Soon, I'll sink
my teeth in slowly, as slow as the sun
sets in July, the light, bright fireflies
popping on my tongue.
Juice dribbling down my chin
as if from a peach
in a poem about water
dropping off my paddle
early in the morning, in the
cool, dark lake pockets where the herons
fish and the turtles sleep.

Or maybe I'll slice it,
cool and crisp as the crack
of a bat as the crowd goes wild,
and set it on a slice of white
bread with a slather of shimmering
mayonnaise that plays with the rays
of the sun like the oil on the old
ladies laying in the sand, like the water
itself.

Put it on a plate, perhaps,
with a cut-up cucumber,
vinegar and a sliver of onion
for that tang, that zip
of the tent with the sliver
of moon in the sky, the air thick
with humidity, waiting to be wrung
of summer like a tomato
on the counter.

Meditations on a Token That Is a Seed

I.
This seed will never be
something else. It does, however,
possess a sheen of light
from somewhere else.

II.
Its metallic smell is not unlike
the water from the shower
in a cabin deep in the woods.

II.
It knows the hearts of three people:
the One who made it
the One for whom
it was made
and the One
into whose hands it fell. / to whom it was given

III.
It waits, silent and still,
to see what we might nurture;
what will become of our
coming and going.

IV.
In it are the familiar lines,
strokes and gestures
of the man
whose hands
gave it shape.
It may belong to me, but it will always be His.

V.
It is practically useless.
Its only purpose is metaphor,
which is to say:

beauty.
Its function is invaluable.

VI.
The concentrated weight of it
in my fingers, in my pocket,
is an anchor on the end
of a very long line.

VII.
There is something growing from the seed.
This may be less important than the heart of germination.

VIII.
Remember when the seed passed
from one to another?
How desperate we were, and unsure.

IX.
The seed is both a gate
and a beginning.
It is an icon.

X.
It is not to be worshipped, the seed.
Or is it?

XI.
It is a choice.

XII.
The seed lives among strings of beads,
bottles of perfume, and the smallest,
most luminous rocks.
They belong together,
like the jewelweed, the hellbender
and the stump upon which we may sit.

That Letters Make Words

One by one, we turn the tiles face down, mute,
dumb with power. We draw them in, fifteen each,
to see what they might say;
to see if they're enough
to carry us across this sororal equinox:
we have known each other
exactly as long as we haven't.
Oh, that letters make words make
truths make bonds that bridge gaps in years.

We spent our college days decoupaging
our journals, sneaking into the bell tower
and sending each other big boxes of letters
from faraway places that we'd read
on the rec fields, letting the moonlight touch
our pale bodies, making lists of things
we wanted from life and love.

Blink one eye, and half our lives
have passed. Squint the other,
and they've doubled. There's so much
to say, now, so many years
and babies and babies wanted
and never had and never will
and fought for and fought over
and not missed at all

and sex that's more complicated
than we were led to believe,
depressed husbands and recovered husbands,
partners in the program and partners
who will become husbands or won't,
and husbands who just need
to breathe.

And it's all there, it could be, spread out on the table
between us, tiles and tears in sparkling pools
beneath our hearts. One by one, we turn over letters,
arrange and rearrange searching for words, the right words,
to span unspoken years,
and I keep turning them over and over,
letter by letter, turning, turning.

Uncaged

The dog is outside and you are almost home.
I should get up from where I sit
bathing in sunlight and skin and words
and call him in so that he doesn't make a mad dash
for freedom
when you open the gate.
I believe I shan't.
Not because I'm lazy
or tired of wiping his paws in the rain
but because I want you to find me here
your non-wife,
waiting for you
like an animal
who stays.

I See Her in All the Places She Isn't

It was February when I saw them for the first time:
skeletons, on the tips of the branches
of the tree next door. 100 years old at least,
it rose to the bedroom window and beyond,
so when the watery green leaves appeared
like lily pads, and we covered the walls
with Willow Wind and Summer Mist, we'd kneel
at the headboard and peer out the window
into the depths
where there were only dry bones, before
and point out the tulips
as if they were lotuses,
our bed a canoe.

Every morning, a silent movie played
like a dream on still-drawn shades:
bobbing branches as lazy fish,
cat happy-napping on my pillow below.

The tree waved at itself in the heavy mirror
we hung over the dresser; I picked out my jewelry
and it was in front of me. It was behind me.
We swam in this tree.

In the room downstairs with the blue paint,
the light from the strange window that spans the wall
above our heads reaches just high enough to
kiss the bottom-most boughs. It was as if
we floated on our backs in a cold lake in July,
bobbing on the waves as the water ever so often
slips over our eyes, and we didn't even feel it
beneath us

her eyes were so blue

The limbs came down first,
and the tree shrank
from the outside in,
like she did,
until it was nothing
but its trunk,
thick with age,
still magnificent,
even leafless, limbless.
The dishes rattled when it fell.
There's only air where it was

      where she was

At the Rothko Chapel the Day Before

Black
that holds light,
the quality of warmth,
enough to be more
than simply dark.
Four walls, or probably
more--there were nooks,
surely--and was there
a window in the ceiling?
Where did the light come from?
It's the details that fall away.
We sat apart, that much
I know. I know the sound of my sniffling
touched each of the not-quite-black
walls.

One Day Begins the Greening (It's In the Roots)

It's in the way, after a long winter
in which the bleak and barren
seem to have no end—let alone a beginning—
one day begins the greening. There, on the tips
of the trees and fluttering a rabbit's nose
above the ground, a suggestion. Of renewal,
you might think, but no: persistence. Because then
comes another, and there is all of life, again,
all of color, of warmth, all growing, all blossoming,
all love, all light, and is it a miracle? Does the heady scent
of petrichor have you believing all is made new?
This is the truth: when, consumed by darkness,
your path disappears before you, just then
the earth churns its important work, beneath
your feet, feeding the fount of Spring's first flower;
the one who waits until the ground is soft enough
to push though, tenderly at first—a rabbit's nibble—
and lift its purple head, bobbing, nodding you forward.

Notes:

The poem, "It Takes Twelve Seconds to Beat Egg Whites Fairly Stiff at Home with a Mixer" references Ross Gay's poem, "An Ode to Sleeping in My Clothes," from his book, *Catalog of Unabashed Gratitude* (University of Pittsburgh Press, 2015).

"Meditations on a Token that Is a Seed" is after Wallace Stevens' "13 Ways of Looking at a Blackbird."

Abby Wheeler was born and raised by the river in New Richmond, Ohio. She now lives in Cincinnati, where she is a staff and community member at Women Writing for (a) Change.

www.ingramcontent.com/pod-product-compliance
Lightning Source LLC
LaVergne TN
LVHW041507070426
835507LV00012B/1384